THE STORY OF THE EARTH
DESERT

LIONEL BENDER

FRANKLIN WATTS

New York · London · Toronto · Sydney

© 1989 Franklin Watts

First published in the USA by
Franklin Watts Inc.
387 Park Avenue South
New York. N.Y. 10016

US ISBN: 0 531 10707 8
Library of Congress Catalog Card
No: 87 51612

Printed in Belgium

Consultant Dougal Dixon

Designed by Ben White

Picture research by Jan Croot

Prepared by Lionheart Books
10 Chelmsford Square
London NW10 3AR

Illustrations:
Peter Bull Art

Photographs
L. Bender 12
GeoScience Features *cover*, 1, 7, 10, 17, 20, 25, 29
Heather Angel 14
Hutchinson Library 8, 13, 21, 22, 24
Robert Harding 23, 31, 27
Survival Anglia 19
Dr A. C. Waltham 11
ZEFA 28

THE STORY OF THE EARTH
DESERT

LIONEL BENDER

CONTENTS

This book tells the story of a typical desert. It explains how the desert and its landscape features are formed. Some deserts in the world are sandy and others are stony. Deserts are always changing, and a sandy desert may one day become a bare area of rock. All deserts, though, are very dry areas of land.

▽ The illustration shows the complete story of our desert. The desert is sheltered from wet winds by mountains. When rain does fall, it washes down loose rocks on to the flat land below. The water collects in lakes that quickly dry out, or it comes to the surface in pools. Winds blowing over the desert carry sand. They wear away rocks into odd shapes.

The dry air of the desert causes the soil to crumble into sand. The sand blows about in the wind with such force that rocks are worn away by it, forming more sand. The sand may gather in "seas", with mounds of sand stretching as far as the eye can see. These mounds, or dunes, may be blown away in storms, leaving a bare rocky area.

▽ We have divided the story of our desert into ten stages. In the following pages of the book we look at each stage in turn. There are photographs of deserts in different parts of the world. Diagrams explain how the different features of a desert are formed. We also look at the plants and animals of deserts and how deserts affect people in various parts of the world.

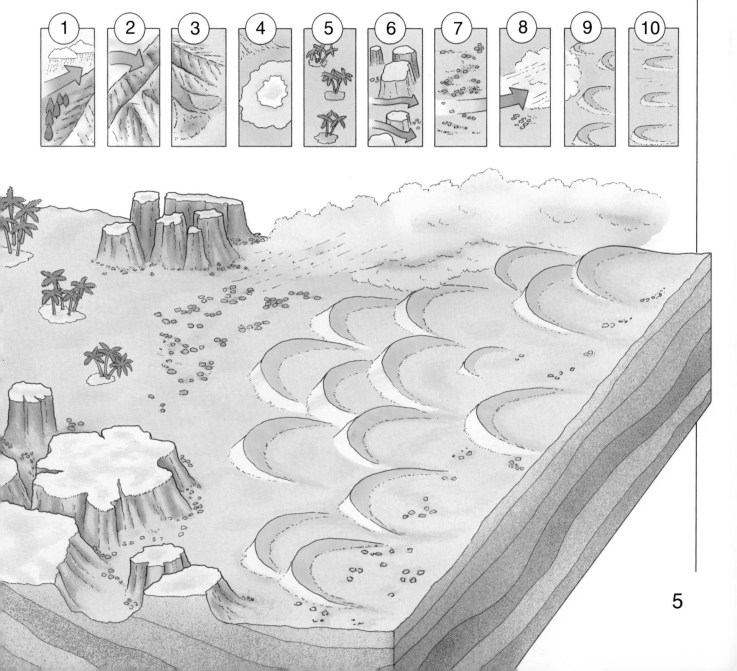

As winds blow across the seas, they pick up moisture. This moisture usually falls as rain over the land. Where there are mountains near the sea, the winds blow up the mountainsides and drop all the rain along the coast. Then, only dry winds blow over the mountaintops and over the land beyond. These dry winds create deserts.

Deserts also form where the winds are always dry, either because they blow from the land to the sea, or because they are far from any sea.

▷ The dry desert winds must have lost their moisture somewhere. We can sometimes see the moisture as rain clouds around a mountaintop, or as dampness in lush forests growing on hills facing the sea. This damp forest of ferns and moss-covered trees is on coastal hills on one of the Seychelles Islands off the east coast of Africa.

▽ As air rises, it cools. As it cools, its moisture collects as drops of rain. Moist winds blowing off the sea give wet weather on mountain slopes along the coasts of land masses, or continents. The dry winds that blow beyond the mountains create a type of desert known as a rain shadow desert.

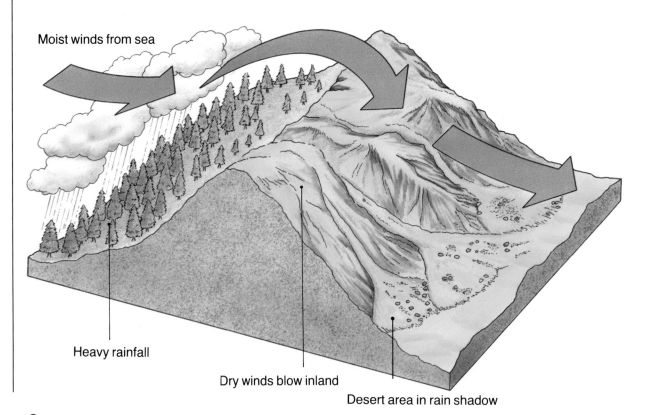

Moist winds from sea

Heavy rainfall

Dry winds blow inland

Desert area in rain shadow

The desert is not dry all the time. A few inches of rain may fall each year. But this rain usually falls in just one day, and as a single sudden downpour. It falls with such force that great floods of water rush down valleys, wearing away deep grooves, or gorges, in the land.

A dry area of land cut by gorges is impossible to farm, and vehicles cannot easily cross it. Such a barren area is given the name badlands. Most deserts start life as badlands.

◁ A badland is a landscape of dry gorges and ridges. It is formed by the rains that fall in a few days each year or perhaps only once every few years. This badland is at Zabriskie Point in Death Valley, California.

▽ Desert rains usually come from thunderstorms. In flat desert areas, the rain quickly soaks into the ground. But where there are steep slopes, the water collects in channels and gushes downhill. These "flash floods" create valleys with flat floors and steep sides. These wide gashes in desert slopes are known as wadis. Wadis are dry for most of the year.

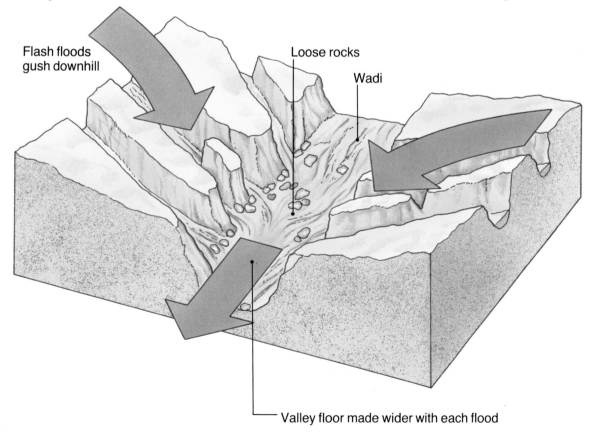

Flash floods gush downhill

Loose rocks

Wadi

Valley floor made wider with each flood

9

Flash floods scoop out rocks, boulders and pebbles from the floors of the wadis. The fast-flowing waters carry these chunks of rock downhill. As the force of the water weakens, the chunks fall to the ground.

The heavy boulders come to a halt first. The lighter pebbles are carried farthest by the flood waters. They are dumped on the ground where the wadis open out on to flat land known as the desert plain.

▷ At the end of a wadi the water currents in a flash flood slow down as the water spreads out over the land and seeps underground. The pebbles, gravel and stones carried by the water collect in a cone- or fan-shaped mass, as here in California.

▽ The water in this flash flood in a desert in southern Iran is brown, thick and murky with the rock pieces that it carries along.

The water that comes down from the hills in flash floods usually soaks into the land. Where it cannot easily flow away, it gathers in huge lakes, which slowly dry up in the Sun. As they dry up, chemicals that are in the water, such as salt from the rocks, collect in large amounts.

The water becomes more and more salty. Gradually, the salt gathers at the bottom of the lake. When the lake dries out completely, a thick layer of salt is left on the desert surface.

▷ Death Valley, California, is a desert region that lies below sea level. Flood waters flowing down from the surrounding hills cannot flow away. They become trapped in the valley to form a lake. Each time the lake dries out a layer of salt builds up in the valley. Eventually, a vast dazzling "salt pan," or playa, forms.

◁ Flood water passing over rocks washes away some of the chemicals they contain.

In desert lakes, the water is heated by the Sun and turns to vapor. The chemicals form masses of large crystals on the bed of the lakes. These become "baked" hard by the Sun – hard enough to drive over.

Still some water

The surface of the desert is very dry. However, there is plenty of water beneath it. Some layers of rock are like sponges – they are full of tiny holes that can fill with water. These layers are known as aquifers, from the Latin word *aqua* meaning water. Following a flash flood, an aquifer becomes filled with water. In places, the aquifer lies near the desert surface and creates a small, damp area, or oasis, in the sandy wasteland.

◁ A patch of plants, such as palm trees, growing in the middle of a desert is a welcoming sight. It is an oasis, which means food and drink to desert travelers and their animals. This oasis is at Huacachina in the Peruvian Desert.

▽ An aquifer may receive its water from rains that have fallen on distant mountains. The aquifer may be a continuous layer of rock under large areas of the desert. Sometimes, if the rock layer is cracked, or faulted, the water seeps to the surface. In other places the aquifer may stick out at the surface. In both cases, the moisture in the rock provides water for plants to grow, and an oasis forms.

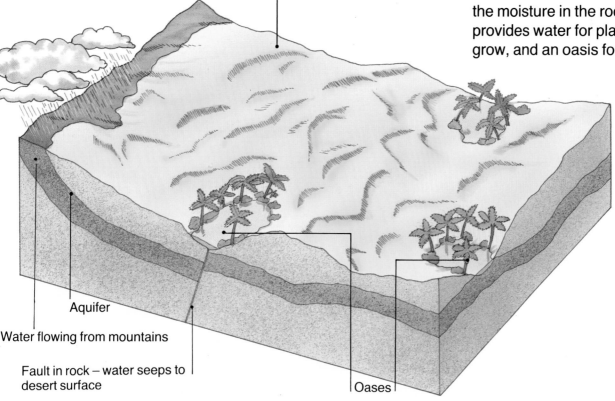

Dry rock and sand

Aquifer

Water flowing from mountains

Fault in rock – water seeps to desert surface

Oases

Desert wildlife

A desert is a difficult place in which to live. There is little to eat and water cannot be found easily. During the day, the Sun beats down fiercely from a cloudless sky, and temperatures can reach 55°C (131°F). At night, it can be extremely cold. Despite the harsh conditions, many kinds of animals and plants live in deserts. Some animals spend their entire lives here.

▽ Desert plants may have roots that are 20 m (66 ft) long. These reach down to the aquifer. Some plants, like cacti, store water in their thick fleshy stems and so can survive months or years without water. Animals such as ground squirrels and desert rats hide away in burrows from the worst heat of the day. Even Sun-loving creatures like lizards only come out in the morning and evening when the weather is cooler.

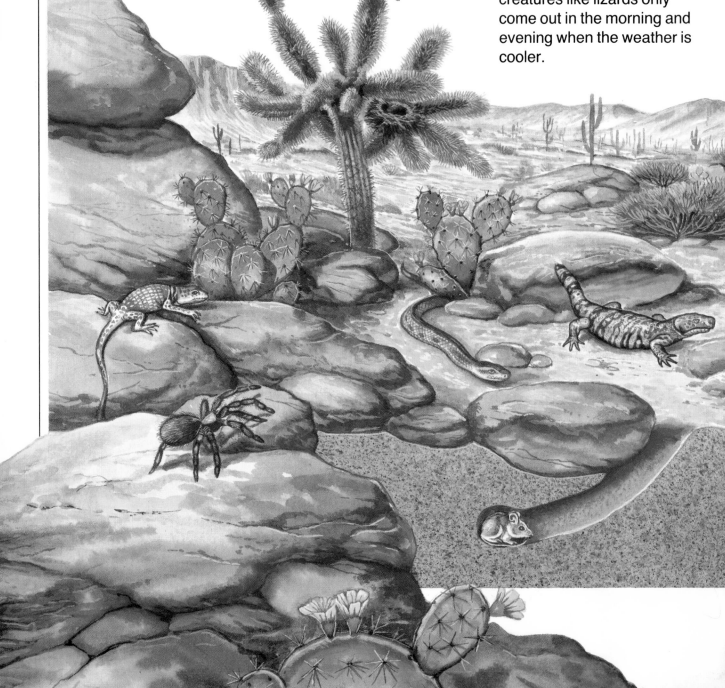

▷ The rattlesnake of the Mojave Desert, California, is a typical hunting desert animal. It does not drink, but gets its water from the moist flesh of the small animals that it eats. The small animals do not drink either, but gain their water from the seeds and stems of the desert plants on which they feed.

As winds blow across the open spaces of the desert, they pick up grains of dry sand and carry them along. The grains bounce over the ground and swirl up high into the air. The sand is blasted along with such force that it wears away, or erodes, the rocks in its path.

Over thousands of years, large chunks of desert rock are carved into strange shapes by the sand and wind. The rock that is worn away turns to yet more sand, and so the carving process continues.

▷ Where a narrow ridge of rock sticks up in the desert, the wind and swirling sand often wear away hollows in each side of it. Eventually, they may wear right through the rock and form an arch, like this one, known as Delicate Arch, in Utah.

▽ Flat-topped hills eroded out of desert rocks are called mesas, or tables. As the sides of mesas are worn away by the windblown sand, the hills become columns of rock. These desert columns are known as buttes.

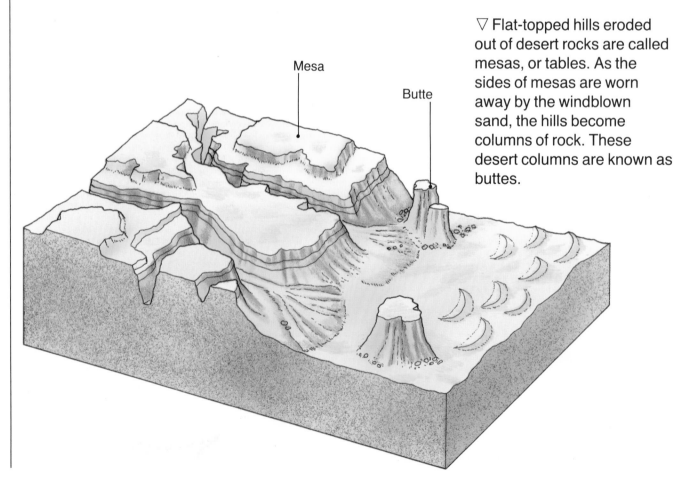

Mesa

Butte

The rocks of the desert surface are continuously heated during the day and then frozen at night. This causes them to break up into boulders, pebbles, sand and dust. The lighter parts – the sand and the dust – are blown away by the wind and form sand mounds, or dunes. The heavier boulders and pebbles are left behind, and form a rubbly surface known as desert pavement, or reg. Underneath the pavement there is still plenty of sand and dust, but it is now sealed off from the wind. A rock desert is formed.

▽ In most deserts, rocky pavement areas are more common than sandy areas. Here, in the desert of Dasht-e-Lut in eastern Iran, mile after mile of stony ground stretches out in all directions.

△ In this desert area of Libya, North Africa, the wind has blown away the sand from between the stones. It has also worn smooth the stones where they lie. Some of the stones will be worn flat on one side and they may then topple over. The other side of the stones may be eroded away until flat. The desert pavement will then be filled with flat-sided stones, which are known as dreikanters.

Strong winds blowing across the desert pavement may pick up so much loose rock material that they form thick clouds of sand. These roll across the desert surface like huge, dark waves. Such sandstorms blot out the Sun and, like a fog, make it impossible to see very far in the desert.

When the wind swirls about wildly, the sand is caught up in swaying, dancing columns called dust devils. These have a scouring, or sand-blasting, effect on the landscape.

◁ Strong winds sweep the sand from the tops of dunes and blow it along a few feet above the ground. Sandstorms, such as this one in Dasht-e-Kavir, Iran, make desert travel difficult.

△ ▷ The sand-blasting effect of sandstorms often creates mushroom-shaped, or pedestal, rocks. These are known as zeugens.

The rubbly surface of the desert pavement is partially covered by sand that has been dropped by the winds. These patches form isolated sand dunes. Along the edges of the pavement so many dunes form that they merge into one large area of sand.

Eventually, the sand forms a continuous layer, like a sea of water, and the desert pavement becomes completely covered in dunes.

▷ In a sandy desert, huge dunes, many kilometres long, contain smaller dunes and tiny sand ripples. The whole sandy surface is called a sand sea, or erg. This sand sea is Erg Chech in the Sahara Desert, Africa.

◁ In a sand sea, each dune slopes gently upward in the same direction as the winds blow. The winds push sand grains up this slope and drops them down the other, steeper, side of the dune. Over many weeks or months, the whole dune rolls across the desert surface, just as a wave moves over the seas and oceans when pushed by the winds.

Over thousands of years, all the sand is blown away from the area. Only bare rock is left. Where once there were mountains, now there is a gently sloping rocky surface called a pediment.

The mountains have been worn down to this level by the flash floods and the sand-blasting of the winds. In places, masses of tough rock, which are not easily worn down by the weather, stand as isolated rounded hills. These are called inselbergs, meaning island mountains.

▷ Inselbergs stick up above the level of the pediment like islands above the surface of the oceans. They are worn down by the wind very slowly, layer by layer. They usually have a rounded appearance.

This photo shows one of the world's most famous inselbergs, Ayers Rock, which is in central Australia.

▽ The surface rock of a desert area is eventually worn flat to form a pediment. In some places the pediment may be covered by thin patches of gravel, as here in the Tassili n'Ajjer region of the Sahara Desert of Algeria.

Deserts and people

Many peoples of the world live in desert areas. Some, like the Kurds of Central Asia and the Bedouin of North Africa, graze sheep and goats on the plants that grow in the rainy seasons. They move with their flocks from oasis to oasis as each one dries up. Others, such as the Bushmen of the Kalahari Desert in southern Africa and the Aborigines of Australian deserts, are constantly on the move in search of food and water.

▽ It is difficult, but not impossible, to grow trees in deserts. Here a young tree has been planted in a hollow made in the sand. The tree's roots are kept moist with water constantly dripping from a pipe leading from an oasis.

△ A herd of sheep and goats is moved to the hills from a desert plain in order to graze on a fresh area of grass. In some desert regions of Africa and Asia, too many animals are allowed to feed on the plants. Plant roots hold the soil together, and once they are removed, the soil quickly crumbles and forms sand. Land that could be used to grow crops is rapidly becoming desert waste.

Glossary

Butte An isolated hill or column of rock in a desert area.

Desert Any area of the world that has less than 30 cm (12 in) of rain in a year. Most deserts are in hot regions of the world, where daytime temperatures can reach above 55°C (about 130°F) and rain falls only once a year.

The North Pole and South Pole regions, and the ice fields on the tops of high mountains, are known as "cold deserts."

Dreikanter A stone with flat faces and sharp edges, worn down by the desert wind. The name means three-sided.

Dune A mound or hill of sand that is constantly being moved along in the wind.

Erg A sandy desert consisting of a sea of rolling sand dunes.

Erosion The wearing away of rocks by the action of rain, wind and other weather conditions.

Flash flood A sudden gush of water produced by heavy rainfall in a usually dry area of land.

Inselberg A rounded hill that sticks up like an island in the desert. The name means "island mountain".

Mesa A flat-topped hill in a desert. A mesa is produced when a flat area of land is eroded, or worn away, in sections and the sides are worn away by sudden flooding.

Pediment A desert surface that has been worn down to a bare layer of rock known as the bedrock.

Playa A lake of salty water that dries out in the dry season to form a layer of salt crystals on the surface of the ground.

Reg An area of stony desert, with a surface consisting of rubble. Another name is desert pavement.

Wadi A valley with a flat floor and steep sides that is filled with water only in the wet season.

Zeugen A mushroom-shaped rock formed by the sand-blasting action of desert winds.

Facts about deserts

Biggest temperature difference between night and day A drop from 52°C (126°F) to −2°C (26°F) between midday and midnight has been recorded in the Sahara Desert.

Biggest desert area The main desert belts of the world lie just to the north and the south of the equator, along the tropics of Cancer and Capricorn.

Air that has risen at the equator descends along these belts. This descending air is dry. The Mexican Desert, the Sahara Desert and the Arabian Desert lie along the northern belt.

The Patagonian Desert in South America, the Kalahari Desert in Africa, and the Simpson and Gibson deserts in central Australia lie along the southern belt.

Biggest single desert The Sahara desert is the largest, being 5,150 km (3,200 miles) from east to west and 2,250 km (1,400 miles) from north to south.

Proportion of the Earth's surface affected Almost 33 percent of the land surface is desert. This may rise to 35 percent because of damage caused by farming.

Largest sand dunes The largest sand dunes known are in Algeria. They are something like 5 km (about 3 miles) wide and 430 m (1,410 ft) high, but their sizes are constantly changing as winds blow the sand about.

Longest natural arch Of the wind-eroded features in a desert, natural rock arches are quite common. The longest is Landscape Arch in Arches National Park, Utah. It is 88 m (291 ft) long and 30 m (100 ft) high.

▷ These ancient cave paintings of people and animals are from Tassili, Algeria, which today is a region of the Sahara Desert. They prove that thousands of years ago Tassili was a grassy place and that the desert sands have gradually spread to reach their present-day, much larger, area.

Index

PRINTED IN BELGIUM BY
proost
INTERNATIONAL BOOK PRODUCTION